G000153494

# "THE WISDOM OF Kids"™

**Soula Zavacopoulos**

summersdale

THE WISDOM OF KIDS

Summersdale Publishers Ltd
46 West Street
Chichester
West Sussex
PO19 1RP
UK

www.summersdale.com

Printed and bound in China

ISBN: 978-1-84953-374-4

Substantial discounts on bulk quantities of Summersdale books are available
to corporations, professional associations and other organisations. For details
contact Nicky Douglas by telephone: +44(0)1243 756902, fax: +44(0)1243
786300 or email nicky@summersdale.com.

# INTRODUCTION

For centuries the world's greatest thinkers have been plagued by the Essential Questions of Life, such as, 'What is love?', 'What is the difference between men and women?' and 'Why do grownups get drunk so much?' Who knew that the answers to these conundrums were so simple? We should have been asking our kids all along...

This long-sought knowledge has been painstakingly compiled and is now collected within these pages. At last you can discover how to stop your hair going grey, the importance of wearing the right shoes and why you should always watch out for flying rice pudding at weddings. This endearing and original collection of wise words from little geniuses proves that kids really do say the funniest things.

"Shake your hips
and hope for
the best."

– Camille, age 9

# IF YOU CAN'T REMEMBER YOUR AGE:

" Just look in the back of your pants. Mine say five to six."

— Tina, age 5

# WORST PRESENT
## IN HISTORY...

"The prince bringing
Cinderella a glass shoe.
If it's not a Manolo
Blanket, don't bother."

– Victoria, age 11

# IS IT BETTER TO BE SINGLE OR MARRIED?

"It's better for girls to be single but not for boys cos they need someone to clean up after them."

– Anita, age 9

Shhhhhh!

# anger management techniques:

"If your dad's cross
and asks you,
'Do I look stupid?'
don't answer him."

– Sarah, age 10

# WHAT'S annoyinG aBouT
# BEinG younG?

"I want my hair cut with a hole on top like Daddy's, but he said I've got to wait till I'm older."

– Samir, age 6

"If you get married in church watch out, cos people throw rice pudding at you."

– Tom, age 4

# GETTING YOUR PRIORITIES RIGHT...

"Love is the most important thing in the world, if you don't count football."

– Andrew, age 10

# HOW TO STAY LOOKING YOUNG...

"Ask a vampire to bite your neck, then hit him with garlic & run!"

— Oliver, age 5

"No.

You're a big fat

poo head."

– Sasha, age 3

## COS YOU'RE A SUPER DUPER FRIEND...

"I can remember your birthday WITHOUT a Facebook reminder!"

– Julia, age 12

# WHAT TO DO ON A BAD FIRST DATE:

"I'd run home and play dead. The next day I would call all the newspapers and make sure they wrote about me in all the dead columns."

— Craig, age 9

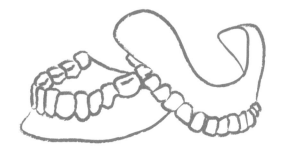

# WHAT CHANGES AS YOU GET OLDER?

" The tooth fairy doesn't give me money anymore. I think she spent it all on Granddad."

– Jessica, age 8

# THE BEST PRESENT FOR a GIRL...

"Boxer chocolates."

– John, age 6

# WHY DO SOME MEN GO BALD?

"Dunno, but if you go too bald people will see what you're thinking."

— Ralph, age 4

# THE DIFFERENCE BETWEEN
## men and women:

"Women have boobies.
They have one for
hot milk and one for
cold milk."

- Michael, age 5

# BEST PLACE TO GO
## on your birthday...

" Buckingham palace,

cos you get to see

the Queen's

private parts."

– Rachel, age 6

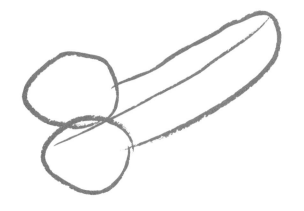

# WeLL, WHAT a LOVELY DrawING

Scissors

— Antonia, age 5

# YOU KNOW IT'S TIME FOR
# BOTOX WHEN...

"Why doesn't
my forehead
bend like yours?"

— Thomas, age 4

# WHY DO GROWNUPS LOVE WINE?

" It helps them live long.
Cos it's grapes it's 1 of
your 5 a day, so basically
it's a health drink."

– Alice, age 6

# HOW TO make someone FALL In LOVe WITH YOU:

"One way is to take the girl out to eat. Make sure it's something she likes. French fries usually works for me."

- Bart, age 9

sorry

**OOOOOPS.**
# I'm sorry!

"It wasn't me,
but I won't
do it again."

— Thomas, age 4

# HOW TO GET A SECOND DATE:

"On the first date just tell each other lies, and that usually gets them interested enough to go for a 2nd date."

-Mike, age 10

# WORST PRESENT IN HISTORY...

"My sister's boyfriend gave her crabs and she dumped him. I think she wanted a kitten."

— Mary, age 10

## WHEN YOU REACH
# a certain age...

"Will my birth certificate expire when I'm as old as you?"

– Daniel, age 5

# BIRTHDAY PRESENTS WOMEN LOVE...

"Jewellery's good, but hambags are better, cos you can eat them."

– James, age 4

# WHY DO PEOPLE GO BALD?

" Cos you grow and grow and grow and one day you're taller than your hair."

– Adrian, age 5

ELLA MORRIS

# PEOPLE GET FORGETFUL WHEN THEY'RE OLD

"Is that why Mummy sews my name in my uniform, so she doesn't forget who I am?"

– Ella, age 6

# Love is...

"Love is when you tell a boy you like his T-shirt, then he wears it every day."

– Sarah, age 10

## WHAT'S THE SECRET TO LOOKING YOUNG?

"Wear a facemask every _night_. An expensive one is best, like from the Disney shop."

– Sam, age 7

# YOU KNOW SOMEONE
# FANCIES YOU IF:

"They give
you the
red smarties."

– Vicky, age 5

# HOW TO STOP HAIR GOING GREY:

"Put some under your pillow. The hairy fairy will leave you £ which you can use to dye it."

– Becky, age 6

# HOW TO HAVE FUN
## ON YOUR BIRTHDAY...

"I had a really big cack. I got it all over my face. It was the best birthday ever."

– Robby, age 7

# WHAT'S THE MORAL OF CINDERELLA?

"Good things happen when you wear the right shoes."

– Sophia, age 10

# WHO IS THE BOSS, mummy or Daddy?

" Daddy is the boss, until Mummy comes home."

– Chloe, age 7

# THE BEST THING ABOUT BIRTHDAYS...

"You can be naughty and nobody says anything!"

– Alexis, age 6

## WHAT ARE THE SIGNS OF AGEING?

"Old people have really huge CDs that they call RECORDS."

— Selina, age 6

# GET INVOLVED!

You have the chance to be part
of our Wisdom of Kids family!

If your child comes out with a corker,
we want to hear about it. If your
quote is included in the range, The
London Studio will send you some
lovely Wisdom of Kids goodies!

To submit your quote, please email
us at info@theLondonStudio.com

To find out more about The Wisdom of Kids
range of cards, gifts and home products,
follow us on Twitter:
@TheLondonStudio

# www.theLondonStudio.com

If you're interested in finding out more about
our humour books, follow us on Twitter:
@SummersdaleLOL

# www.summersdale.com